ORIGAMI DAVID MITCHELL

BARNES & NOBLE

NEW YORK

© 2002 BY IVY PRESS LIMITED

This 2002 edition published by
BARNES & NOBLE, INC.,
by arrangement with Ivy Press

Reprinted in 2007

ISBN 0-7607-3331-7
ISBN 978-0-7607-3331-8

A CIP record for this book is available
from the Library of Congress

Printed in China
Packaging by Winner Print & Packaging

M 10 9 8 7 6 5 4 3

This book was conceived,
designed, and produced by
IVY PRESS
The Old Candlemakers
West Street
Lewes
East Sussex BN7 2NZ

Creative Director PETER BRIDGEWATER

Publisher SOPHIE COLLINS

Editorial Director STEVE LUCK

Design Manager TONY SEDDON

Senior Project Editor REBECCA SARACENO

Designer JANE LANAWAY

Illustrator JOHN WOODCOCK

Contents

About Origami

This nineteenth-century print shows the folding of colored cranes. The crane is a symbol of peace and it is one of the classic patterns in origami.

Origami is a Japanese word that means "folding paper." Every time you fold a letter to insert it into an envelope, or wrap a present, or make a wedge to stop a table rocking, you are doing origami. You are, of course, also doing origami if you fold paper to create recognizable models of animals and birds, toys for children, or decorations for your home. Origami equals paperfolding—it's as easy as that.

There are independent paperfolding traditions in many cultures, but it was in ancient Japan that paperfolding first began to develop into the delicate and intricate craft that we know today. The discovery of the Crane model, in particular, marks a watershed between paperfolding used for practical, ceremonial, and religious purposes, and paperfolding that could be enjoyed as a creative craft activity in its own right.

Our knowledge of the history of origami in Japan is sketchy, and depends almost entirely on information deduced from pictures and prints rather than from written sources. It would seem that the craft of origami originated among those we would define as the "leisured class:" monks attached to Buddhist temples, and the wives and female children of Japanese aristocrats and their Samurai followers. There is also evidence that Geisha hostesses would sometimes fold Cranes to occupy themselves while waiting for their clients to arrive, though the idea that they used origami to entertain their clients is no more than an attractive myth.

Even when interest in origami became widespread, it was still largely confined to female society. Indeed, the great pioneer of modern origami, Akira Yoshizawa—now officially recognized as one of Japan's "living treasures"—could, at first, only get his work published in women's magazines.

△
Origami is prized for the discipline it demands of its makers. Folding a thousand cranes is said to ensure a long and peaceful life.

Like many other aspects of Japanese culture, origami remained largely a secret until after the end of the Second World War, and it was not until the 1960s that it became widely known and appreciated in the West. Since then, paperfolders in many countries, including lots of intellectuals and academics in Japan, have taken to origami with enthusiasm and created thousands of innovative designs in a wide range of creative styles. The projects in this book have been chosen to display the best elements of traditional and modern origami design side by side.

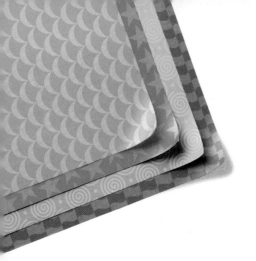

Before You Begin

All you need for origami is...

- a book of designs like this

- some paper

- a hard, flat surface to fold on
- (a kitchen counter, a table, or even a large hardback book resting on your lap will do)

- your hands

- a little patience and determination

- occasionally you will also need a pair of scissors, but usually only to cut the paper down to a smaller size

Most people find that the hardest thing about origami is understanding the diagrams. So here's a quick rundown.

Origami diagrams are drawn as a sequence of "before" and "after" pictures. Each is numbered, so it is easy to read them in the proper order. The "before" picture tells you how a fold is made; the "after" picture shows you the result. Never make a fold until you have looked at the "after" picture to check what the result should be.

Written instructions are always placed near the picture they refer to, and take the same numbers. They use the directions "top," "bottom," "left," "right," "in front," and "behind" in relation to the alignment of the paper and model. The above lefthand diagram explains what these directions mean. The righthand diagrams show the "before" and "after" pictures for a typical fold, together with a detailed explanation of how the fold should be made. Notice that the lefthand corners of

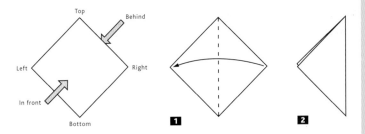

1　　　**2**

the two layers of the paper in step 2 are shown as being slightly offset, even though they should line up exactly. This is confusing but necessary, as it will often be important to know exactly how many layers of paper meet at a point or lie along an edge. Expressed in words, step 1 means, "Fold the righthand corner of the paper across in front so that it lies exactly on top of the lefthand corner, then flatten the fold to form a sharp crease." Step 2 shows the result.

Before folding, make sure that your paper is aligned to match the picture. You will find it is best to flatten the center of the fold first, then work outward to the ends. Most people use their fingernails, but you could equally well use a smooth, hard object, like the rounded handle of a pair of scissors.

If you are a newcomer to the art of origami, it is best to begin by folding the designs at the front of this book. The Cicada is the easiest design of all.

About Paper

Almost any kind of paper can be used for origami. The secret is to match the size, thickness, quality, and decoration of the paper to the requirements of the design you want to fold.

IROGAMI is decorated on one surface but not the other. The undecorated surface is usually white, while the decorated surface may be printed with a simple, plain color, or a pattern.

DYED PAPER is the same color on both surfaces. It usually comes in rectangles rather than squares, so you will need to cut it to shape yourself. Here's an explanation of how to do it.

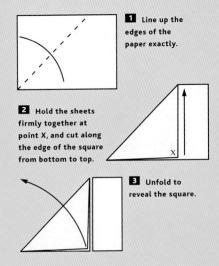

1 Line up the edges of the paper exactly.

2 Hold the sheets firmly together at point X, and cut along the edge of the square from bottom to top.

3 Unfold to reveal the square.

Guide to the Symbols

Before you start...

You will probably find it useful to read through this section before you start to fold, but there is no need to learn the meanings of all the symbols by heart. You can always refer back to this section when necessary.

1 In the diagrams, the edges of the piece of paper are indicated using solid black lines.

2 The direction of the movement arrow tells you which part of the paper moves, and which stays still, as the fold is made. A solid movement arrow indicates that the fold will be made in front of the model.

3 A foldline shows where the new crease will form. A dashed foldline is used when the fold will be made in front of the model.

4 The combination of a dashed foldline and a solid movement arrow tells you the fold is made by folding one part of the paper onto another in front of the model.

5 A movement arrow without a foldline is an instruction to unfold in the direction indicated by the arrow.

6 Creases that have already been made are indicated by thin lines.

7 This version of the movement arrow means fold, crease firmly, then unfold in the direction indicated by the arrow.

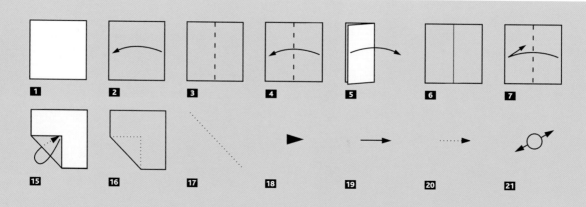

8 A movement arrow with a dotted shaft is used to indicate that a fold will be made behind the model.

9 A dashed and dotted foldline is used to indicate where the crease will form when a fold is to be made behind the model.

10 The combination of a dashed and dotted foldline with a dotted movement arrow tells you a fold is made by folding one part of the paper onto another behind the model.

11 Sometimes the shaft of a movement arrow will be shown partly dotted and partly solid. This instruction means "unfold from behind."

12 This combination of the two kinds of foldlines is used to show you how to collapse the paper into a different shape, using a number of existing creases that run in opposite directions through the paper.

13 When the use of irogami is recommended, shading is used to represent the colored surface of the paper.

14 Shading may also be used to draw attention to some particular part of a model referred to in a written instruction.

15 A symbol of this kind tells you to swivel the flap to the back by reversing the direction of the existing crease.

16 Here, a dotted line is used to show the position of a hidden edge or crease.

17 A dotted line may be used in several other ways: to show the relationship between different parts of the model; to mark the course of a foldline that will produce a crease behind one or more layers of paper; or to show the future position of a particular area of paper that will fall outside the existing boundaries of the model after the fold has been made.

18 A symbol of this kind means that you have to apply gentle pressure to the paper in the direction the arrowhead is pointing.

19 A straight arrow with a solid shaft is used to indicate that you should pull the paper gently in the direction of the arrow.

20 A straight arrow with a dotted shaft is used to indicate that the movement takes place behind one or more layers of paper.

21 This combination of symbols is used to indicate that the relevant layers of the paper must be opened up temporarily, so that a fold can be made between them.

22 This symbol means you need to turn the model over sideways in order to align it with the next picture.

23 This kind of arrow indicates that the next picture has been drawn on a larger scale.

24 A circle may be used to draw your attention to some particularly important part of the model.

25 This combination of symbols is used to introduce intricate folds that affect just one small area of the model. The symbols indicate that the next picture will only show the part of the model inside the circle, but on a much larger scale.

26 This kind of arrow is used when you have to insert the tab of one module inside the pocket of another.

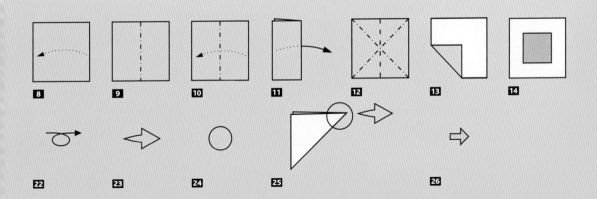

The Cicada

**The Cicada is a very
popular fold in Japan.
There are many variations.
This is one of the simplest.**

The Cicada is a traditional Japanese design. Very few origami designs are as simple and elegant as this, so if you have never done origami before, this is an excellent place to start.

If you choose to use irogami, and begin by placing the colored surface facedown, the back and wings of the Cicada will be marked with broad white stripes. You can vary the folds that produce these stripes to create Cicadas of other species. You can also create white Cicadas with colored markings by beginning with the colored surface faceup.

Paper
You can make
the Cicada from
any kind of paper.

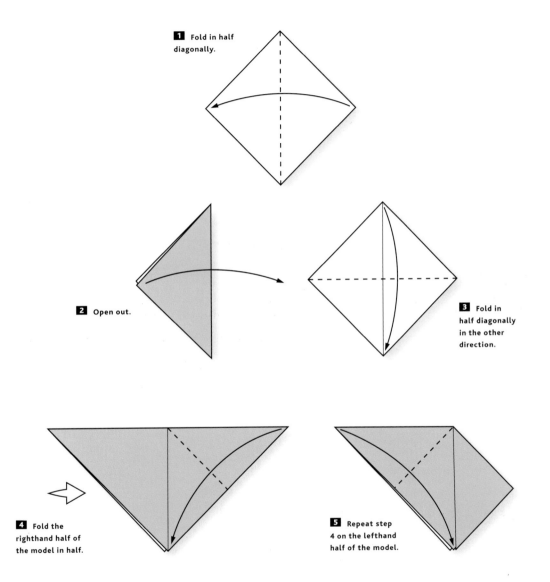

1 Fold in half diagonally.

2 Open out.

3 Fold in half diagonally in the other direction.

4 Fold the righthand half of the model in half.

5 Repeat step 4 on the lefthand half of the model.

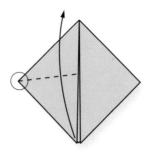

6 The crease that forms this wing must start in the corner highlighted above. Look at step 7 to see the result.

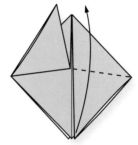

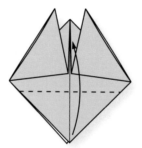

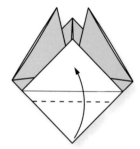

7 Repeat step 6 on the righthand half of the model.

8 This fold is made in just one layer of the paper.

9 This fold is made in the second layer.

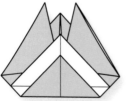

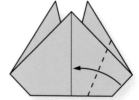

10 Check that your model matches this diagram before moving on.

11 Fold the righthand edge to align with the vertical crease.

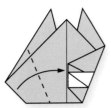

12 Repeat step 11 on the lefthand half of the model.

13 Crease the edges firmly, working in the directions indicated by the arrows.

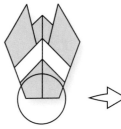

14 Concentrate on the area within the circle.

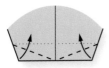

15 The dotted line marks the edge of a hidden layer of paper. The resistance provided by this edge marks one end of each of the next two folds (see step 15); the other ends of the folds originate in the corner of the vertical crease. Make these tiny folds to create the eyes.

16 This is the result.

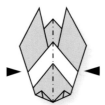

17 Squeeze the sides so that the center rises up in front.

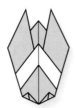

18 The Cicada is finished.

The Kabuto

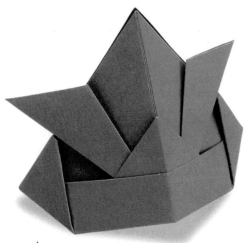

The Kabuto is a traditional Japanese design that represents the horned helmet of a Samurai warrior.

The Kabuto was one of the first traditional designs to become well-known outside Japan. Diagrams for the Kabuto were included in a book of magic tricks, papercuts, and paperfolds that was published in the U.S. in 1922. The title of the book was *Paper Magic,* and the author was none other than the famous conjuror and escapologist, Harry Houdini.

Like the Cicada, the Kabuto is an example of a "pure" origami design—one that is produced by paperfolding alone, without using cuts, glue, or extra decoration beyond the color or pattern of the paper itself. Pure origami is, however, a modern idea; Japanese tradition does not distinguish between models with cuts and those without them.

Paper
The Kabuto should be folded using dyed paper.

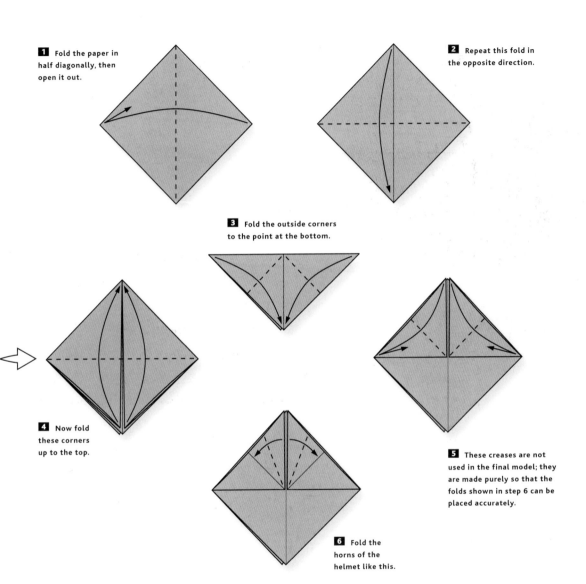

1 Fold the paper in half diagonally, then open it out.

2 Repeat this fold in the opposite direction.

3 Fold the outside corners to the point at the bottom.

4 Now fold these corners up to the top.

5 These creases are not used in the final model; they are made purely so that the folds shown in step 6 can be placed accurately.

6 Fold the horns of the helmet like this.

7 The dotted line shows you how to place this fold.

8 This fold only affects the top two layers.

9 Check that your model looks like this before moving on.

10 Don't forget to crease all your folds firmly.

11 Turn the model over sideways.

12 Squeeze the model so that the center opens up in front and behind.

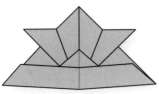

13 This is the simplest version of the Kabuto. Steps 14 through 19 show you how to improve on it.

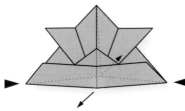

14 Squeeze the lefthand and righthand corners together until they meet in the center and the model lies flat.

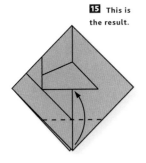

15 This is the result.

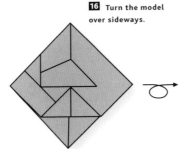

16 Turn the model over sideways.

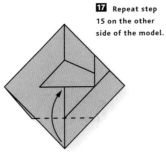

17 Repeat step 15 on the other side of the model.

18 Squeeze the lefthand and righthand corners together so that the center opens up in front and behind. Continue squeezing until the corners meet in the center. The result should look like step 19.

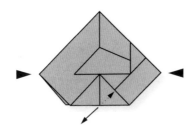

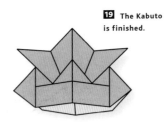

19 The Kabuto is finished.

The Windmill

Paper

The Windmill can be folded using any kind of paper.

The Windmill is a traditional model in its own right, but it can also be used as a base from which many other designs can be developed. Two of these designs, Bric-a-brac and the Floral Giftbox, are included on pages 70–73 and 78–81.

The Windmill can be transformed easily into several other traditional models, including the traditional Spanish "Pajarita," and the ubiquitous Fortune Teller, which you probably learned to fold and decorate at school. If you like manipulative puzzles, you might like to try your hand at discovering (or possibly remembering) how to do this for yourself. You won't need to make any new creases in the paper; just rearrange those that are already there.

The Windmill is not only a traditional design in its own right, but also a base from which other models can be developed.

1 Fold in half diagonally both ways. Open out both times.

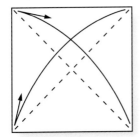

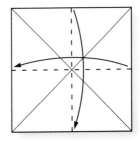

2 Fold in half horizontally and vertically. Open out both times.

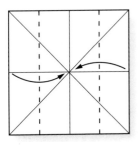

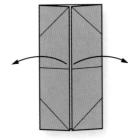

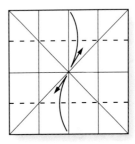

3 Fold the left and right edges onto the vertical crease.

4 Try to avoid flattening the creases when you undo these folds.

5 Repeat steps 3 and 4 from the top and bottom.

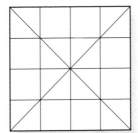

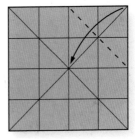

6 Check that you have made all these creases, and turn the paper over.

7 Fold one corner into the center.

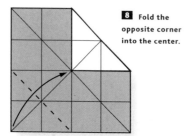

8 Fold the opposite corner into the center.

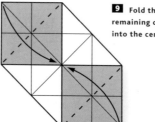

9 Fold the remaining corners into the center.

12 When you first turn the paper over the four corners will be pointing slightly backward. Gently flip each corner forward in turn so that the points identified by circles become concave.

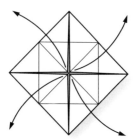

10 Try to avoid flattening the creases when you undo these folds.

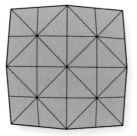

11 Before moving on, check that all these creases are present and correct.

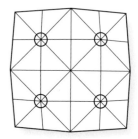

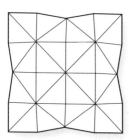

13 The result resembles a shallow dish.

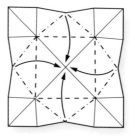

14 Fold the middle of each side into the center of the dish.

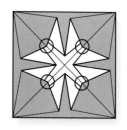

15 Flatten the folds completely so that all the points marked with circles end up in the center.

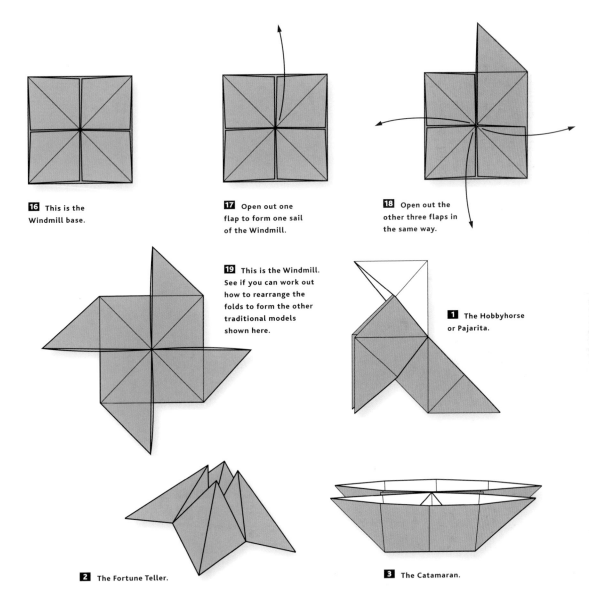

16 This is the Windmill base.

17 Open out one flap to form one sail of the Windmill.

18 Open out the other three flaps in the same way.

19 This is the Windmill. See if you can work out how to rearrange the folds to form the other traditional models shown here.

1 The Hobbyhorse or Pajarita.

2 The Fortune Teller.

3 The Catamaran.

The Coy Carp and Traditional Goldfish

The Coy Carp was discovered by Oliver Zachary

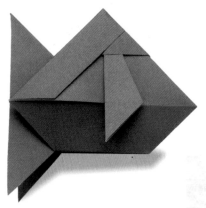

The Goldfish is a traditional Japanese design, and nothing could be less like a fish than the Kabuto, and yet—with the help of two small, strategically placed cuts—the surprising transformation from Samurai helmet to Goldfish can be made.

Despite the fact that many thousands of paperfolders have folded and experimented with the traditional designs over many years, strange discoveries of a similar kind are still there to be made. Shortly before this book was written, a different fish was discovered hiding shyly in the pattern of the folds. The Coy Carp makes its debut here.

Paper

The Coy Carp and Goldfish should be folded using dyed paper.

△
The Coy Carp and the Goldfish are both developed from the Kabuto. One design is traditional, the other brand new.

The Coy Carp

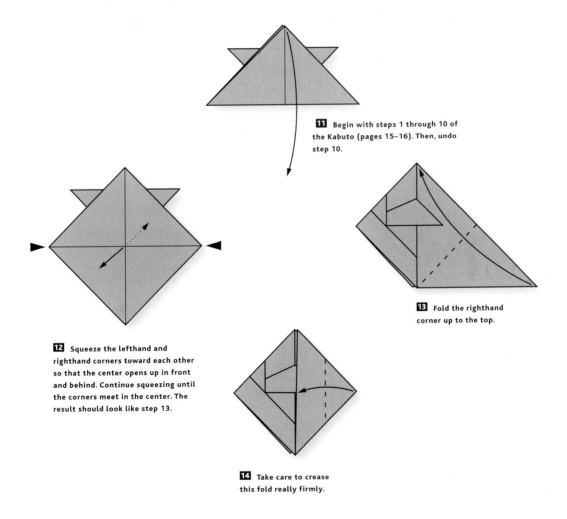

11 Begin with steps 1 through 10 of the Kabuto (pages 15–16). Then, undo step 10.

12 Squeeze the lefthand and righthand corners toward each other so that the center opens up in front and behind. Continue squeezing until the corners meet in the center. The result should look like step 13.

13 Fold the righthand corner up to the top.

14 Take care to crease this fold really firmly.

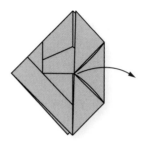

15 Unfold step 14.

16 Undo step 13.

17 Cut along the crease marked with a thick black line. Make sure you only cut through the front layer of the paper.

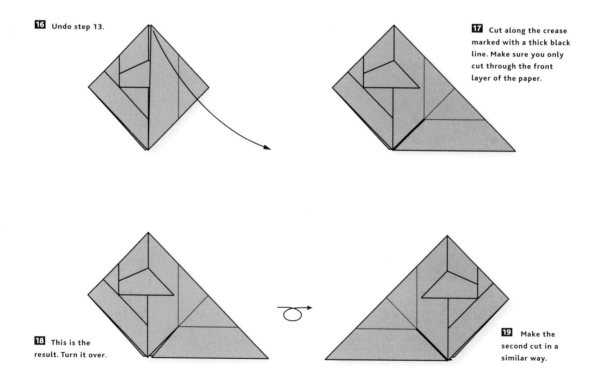

18 This is the result. Turn it over.

19 Make the second cut in a similar way.

20 Separate the front and back layers at point X, and gently push the area identified by the darker shading completely inside out so that point Y ends up at point Z.

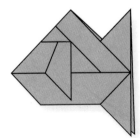

21 Rotate 90 degrees counterclockwise.

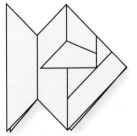

22 The Coy Carp is finished. It can be displayed resting on a small box or on the edge of a shelf.

The Traditional Goldfish

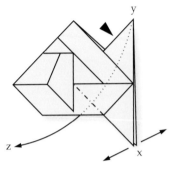

23 Begin with the Coy Carp. Separate the front and back layers at point X and turn the tail inside out so that point Y ends up at Z. The dashed and dotted foldline marks the line of the fold. This fold only affects the inner layers of the model.

24 Rotate 90 degrees clockwise, so that it looks like a fish.

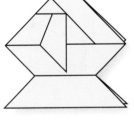

25 The Goldfish is finished. With practice, you will be able to transform the Coy Carp into the Goldfish in one clean movement.

The Spinner

△

The Spinner is made from two square sheets of paper that fit together to form a fascinating spinning toy.

Some origami designs, especially simple toys, seem to spring into existence in many locations simultaneously. The Spinner is a good example. Is it traditional or modern? Japanese, American, or European? Nobody seems to know for sure.

The Spinner is easy to make, great fun to play with, and folds flat so that you can carry it around inside a book, a wallet, or a purse. You can use it as a mobile ornament too.

Most simple origami toys are made from only one square of paper, but the Spinner is made from two. Both squares are folded in exactly the same way, then combined to create the model. The Spinner looks best if each square is a different bright color.

Paper

The Spinner can be folded using any kind of paper.

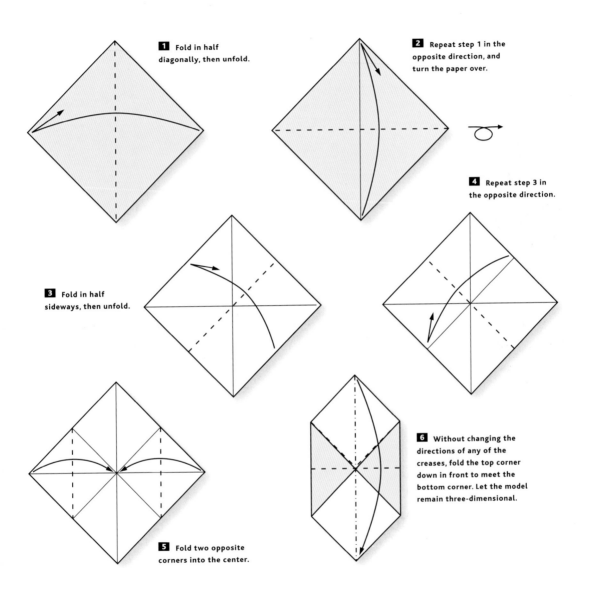

1 Fold in half diagonally, then unfold.

2 Repeat step 1 in the opposite direction, and turn the paper over.

4 Repeat step 3 in the opposite direction.

3 Fold in half sideways, then unfold.

5 Fold two opposite corners into the center.

6 Without changing the directions of any of the creases, fold the top corner down in front to meet the bottom corner. Let the model remain three-dimensional.

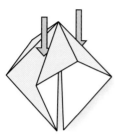

7 The result should look like this. Fold both sheets of paper to this stage.

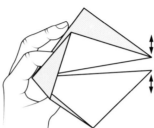

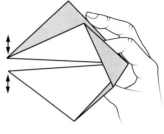

8 Take one of the modules in each hand by inserting the thumb and index finger into the gaps on either side. Be very gentle. The natural spring in the creases will let you treat the modules as simple snapping toys.

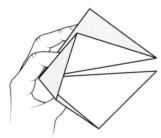

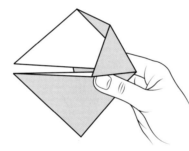

9 Rotate the righthand module through 90 degrees and then bring the two modules together so that the jaws interlock.

10 Halfway there.

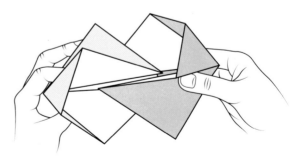

11 Slide the two halves completely together.

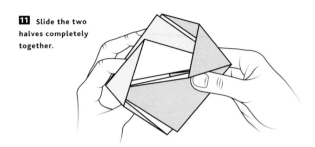

12 Work around the model, pushing all four outside corners into the center of the model as far as they will go.

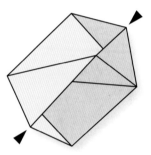

13 This is the result. The Spinner is finished.

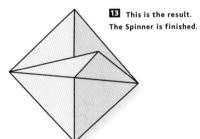

14 Hold the Spinner between the palms of your cupped hands like this and blow gently at the top of the model. The Spinner will spin.

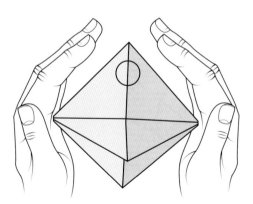

Polly's Parrot

Designed by Polly Smith

▷

Polly's Parrot is an appealing modern design, developed in easy stages from a traditional Japanese base.

Paper

Polly's Parrot can be folded using any kind of paper. Using colorfully decorated irogami will provide the bright plumage the design deserves.

Polly's Parrot is a straightforward modern design that is based, appropriately enough, on a traditional configuration of folds known as the "bird base." This is undoubtedly the most versatile base in origami, and can be developed into a huge variety of designs: particularly models of birds and animals, but also human figures, decorations, containers, and other forms that are more esoteric. Three bird-base designs—all birds, but birds of very different styles and appearance—are included in this book: see pages 34–7, and 38–41 for other two.

Polly's Parrot can be used as a decoration to enhance letters and homemade greetings cards, or as a mobile ornament.

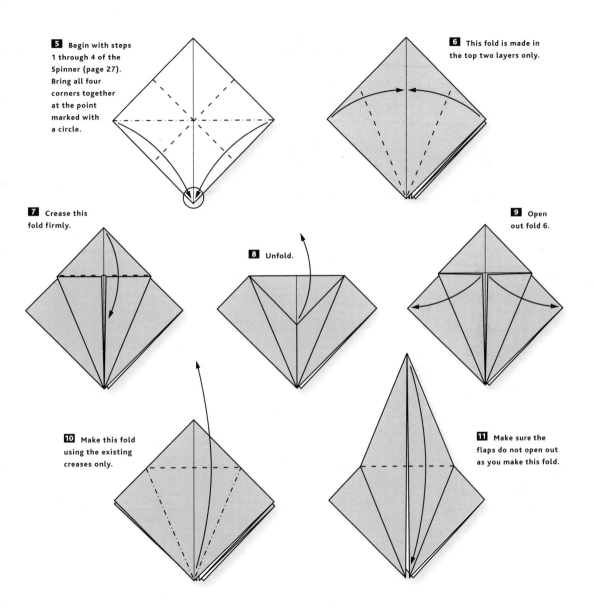

5 Begin with steps 1 through 4 of the Spinner (page 27). Bring all four corners together at the point marked with a circle.

6 This fold is made in the top two layers only.

7 Crease this fold firmly.

8 Unfold.

9 Open out fold 6.

10 Make this fold using the existing creases only.

11 Make sure the flaps do not open out as you make this fold.

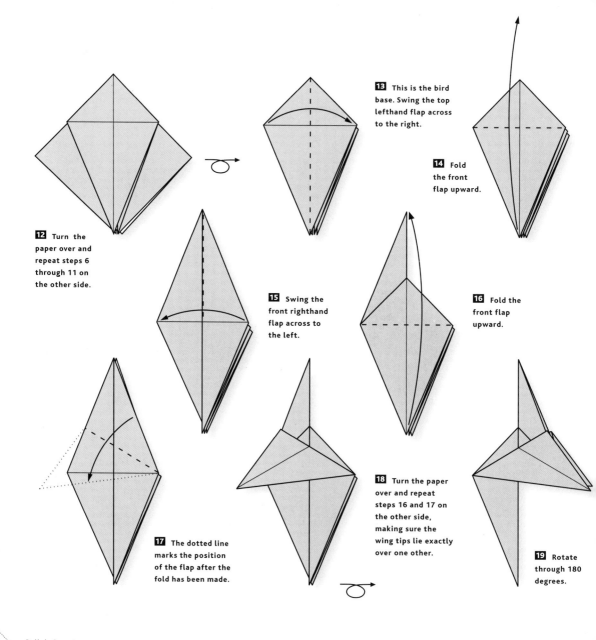

13 This is the bird base. Swing the top lefthand flap across to the right.

14 Fold the front flap upward.

12 Turn the paper over and repeat steps 6 through 11 on the other side.

15 Swing the front righthand flap across to the left.

16 Fold the front flap upward.

17 The dotted line marks the position of the flap after the fold has been made.

18 Turn the paper over and repeat steps 16 and 17 on the other side, making sure the wing tips lie exactly over one other.

19 Rotate through 180 degrees.

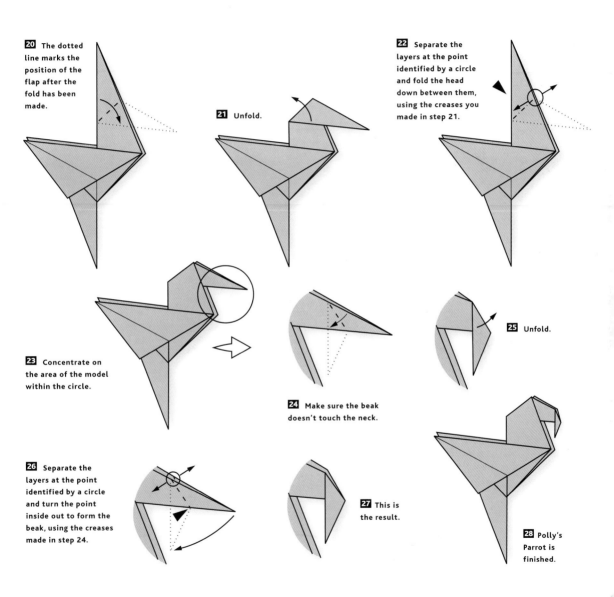

20 The dotted line marks the position of the flap after the fold has been made.

21 Unfold.

22 Separate the layers at the point identified by a circle and fold the head down between them, using the creases you made in step 21.

23 Concentrate on the area of the model within the circle.

24 Make sure the beak doesn't touch the neck.

25 Unfold.

26 Separate the layers at the point identified by a circle and turn the point inside out to form the beak, using the creases made in step 24.

27 This is the result.

28 Polly's Parrot is finished.

The Flapping Bird

The Flapping Bird is
truly a paperfolding
classic. The wings
can be made to flap
by pulling gently on
the tail.

Paper

The Flapping Bird
can be folded
using any kind
of paper.

Leo Tolstoy mentioned the Flapping Bird in his essay "What is Art?," written in 1896. "This winter," he wrote, "a lady of my acquaintance taught me how to make cockerels by folding paper... so that when you pull them by their tails they flap their wings. This invention comes from Japan."

The last statement is particularly interesting because, while the bird base—from which the Flapping Bird is developed—is almost certainly a Japanese invention, the Flapping Bird itself is not at all well known in modern Japan. Perhaps the Flapping Bird has slipped from popularity (and largely from memory too) due to the overwhelming popularity of the Crane? If so, it is a shame. The Crane has much to recommend it, but the Flapping Bird is more elegant and more rewarding to fold.

In these diagrams, the traditional folding method has been varied slightly to make the flapping action more reliable.

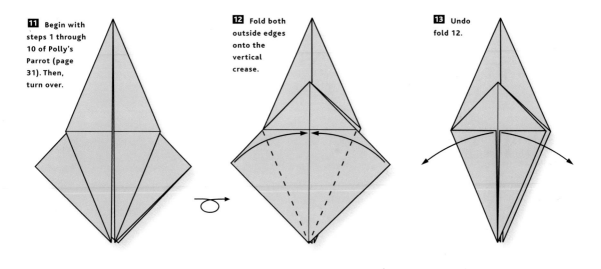

11 Begin with steps 1 through 10 of Polly's Parrot (page 31). Then, turn over.

12 Fold both outside edges onto the vertical crease.

13 Undo fold 12.

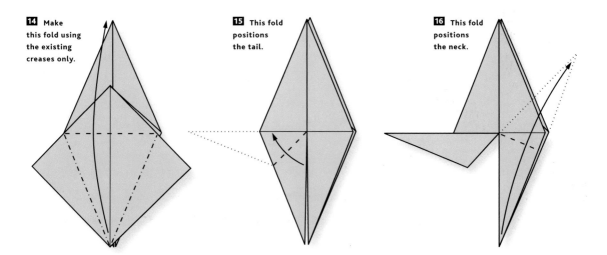

14 Make this fold using the existing creases only.

15 This fold positions the tail.

16 This fold positions the neck.

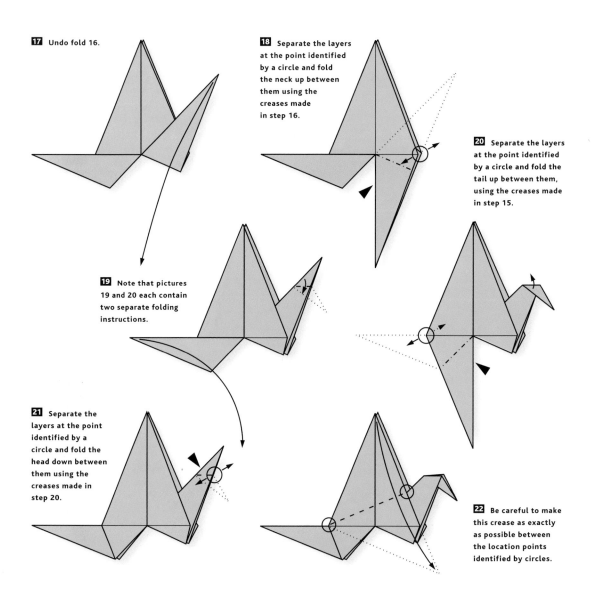

17 Undo fold 16.

18 Separate the layers at the point identified by a circle and fold the neck up between them using the creases made in step 16.

20 Separate the layers at the point identified by a circle and fold the tail up between them, using the creases made in step 15.

19 Note that pictures 19 and 20 each contain two separate folding instructions.

21 Separate the layers at the point identified by a circle and fold the head down between them using the creases made in step 20.

22 Be careful to make this crease as exactly as possible between the location points identified by circles.

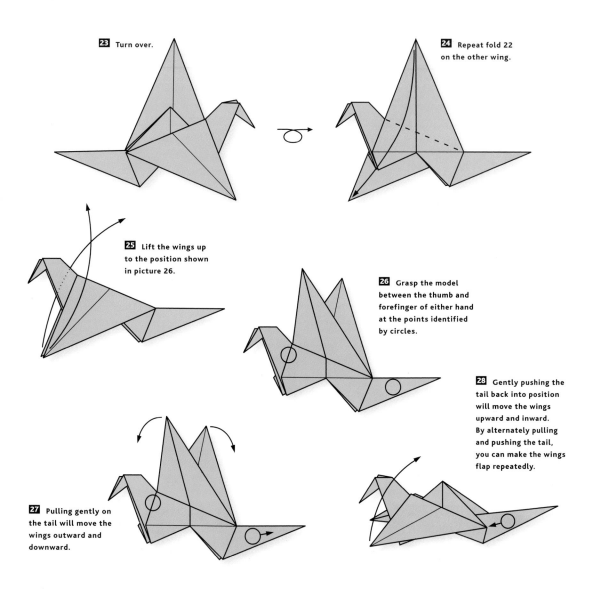

23 Turn over.

24 Repeat fold 22 on the other wing.

25 Lift the wings up to the position shown in picture 26.

26 Grasp the model between the thumb and forefinger of either hand at the points identified by circles.

28 Gently pushing the tail back into position will move the wings upward and inward. By alternately pulling and pushing the tail, you can make the wings flap repeatedly.

27 Pulling gently on the tail will move the wings outward and downward.

The Flying Crane

In modern times, the ever-popular origami crane has become a symbol of international co-operation and peace.

The Flying Crane is a traditional Japanese design. It is undoubtedly the most popular origami design in Japan, and probably in the rest of the world as well.

This is not only due to the merits of the design itself, but because the crane has an important place in Japanese folklore and mythology, and is strongly associated with longevity. Folding a thousand cranes is said to ensure a long and peaceful life.

Despite its popularity, the traditional Flying Crane is not easy to fold well. In these diagrams the traditional folding method has been varied slightly to make it easier to achieve a clean result.

Paper
The Flying Crane can be folded using any kind of paper, but in Japan it is traditionally made from brightly decorated irogami.

15 Begin by following steps 1 through 14 of the Flapping Bird (page 35). Then, fold the point of the righthand edge across in front to lie on the vertical centerline. Look at picture 16: note that the crease does not go all the way to the point at the bottom.

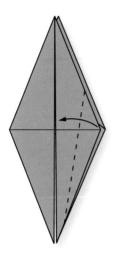

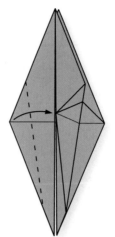

16 Fold the point of the lefthand edge across in front to lie on the vertical centerline in the same place.

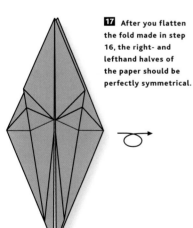

17 After you flatten the fold made in step 16, the right- and lefthand halves of the paper should be perfectly symmetrical.

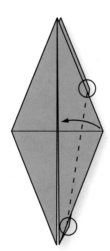

18–19 These folds are a repeat of folds 15 and 16. Make sure that the outside edges line up exactly at the points identified by circles before you flatten the creases.

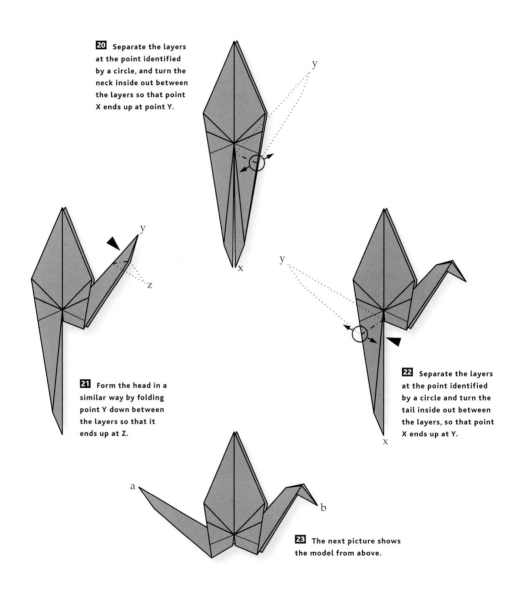

20 Separate the layers at the point identified by a circle, and turn the neck inside out between the layers so that point X ends up at point Y.

21 Form the head in a similar way by folding point Y down between the layers so that it ends up at Z.

22 Separate the layers at the point identified by a circle and turn the tail inside out between the layers, so that point X ends up at Y.

23 The next picture shows the model from above.

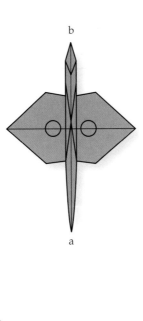

24 Take a wing in each hand, holding them close to the body at the points identified by circles, and gently pull your hands apart. The body of the crane will open out until the model looks like picture 25.

25 Curl the wings to complete the Flying Crane.

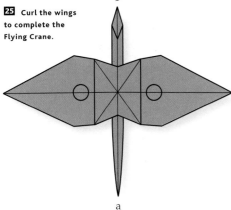

26 The Flying Crane is finished.

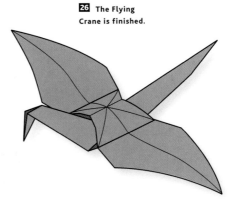

Whippersnapper

Designed by David Mitchell

Paper

Whippersnapper should be folded from dyed paper. Stiff paper works better than thin paper. The more robust the model, the longer it will last.

Whippersnapper is a fine example of an origami action model in which a small movement in one part of the model produces a disproportionately greater movement in another part. In this case, a slight movement of the handles causes the jaws to gape dramatically and snap closed suddenly.

It is one of the joys of origami to make a model like this for a child and to watch them test it to destruction.

Whippersnapper is a challenge to fold, but the amazing action of the snapping jaws is well worth the effort involved.

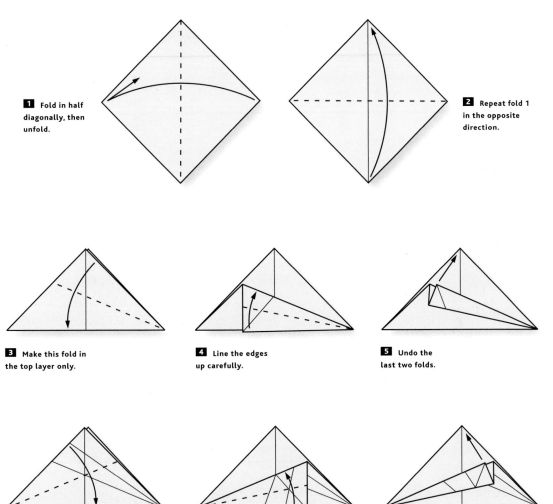

1 Fold in half diagonally, then unfold.

2 Repeat fold 1 in the opposite direction.

3 Make this fold in the top layer only.

4 Line the edges up carefully.

5 Undo the last two folds.

6 Repeat fold 3 in the opposite direction.

7 Line up the edges carefully.

8 Undo the last two folds.

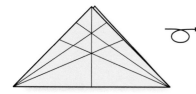

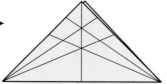

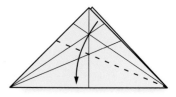

9 Turn over and repeat steps 3 through 8 on the other half of the paper.

10 The front and the back of the model should both now look like this.

11 Make this fold in front...

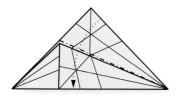

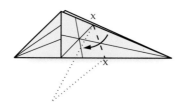

X

X

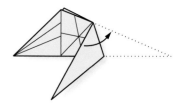

12 ... and this fold behind.

13 Crease XX already exists in the front and back layers of the paper.

14 Unfold.

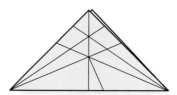

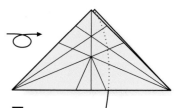

15 Undo folds 11 and 12.

16 Turn over and repeat steps 11 through 15 on the other half of the paper.

17 Open out from behind and rotate 90 degrees clockwise.

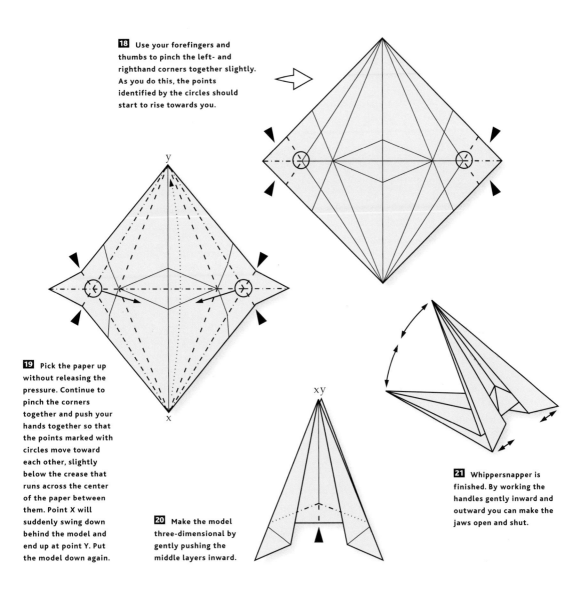

18 Use your forefingers and thumbs to pinch the left- and righthand corners together slightly. As you do this, the points identified by the circles should start to rise towards you.

19 Pick the paper up without releasing the pressure. Continue to pinch the corners together and push your hands together so that the points marked with circles move toward each other, slightly below the crease that runs across the center of the paper between them. Point X will suddenly swing down behind the model and end up at point Y. Put the model down again.

20 Make the model three-dimensional by gently pushing the middle layers inward.

21 Whippersnapper is finished. By working the handles gently inward and outward you can make the jaws open and shut.

Paper

You will need to use paper that is white on one side and overprinted with a bright, light color on the other. Do not use black or very dark paper.

The Windmill Flexagon

Designed by David Mitchell

Flexagons are origami toys that flex to reveal hidden faces. They come in two varieties: the more common version is made by weaving a strip of paper into a flat shape, then joining the two ends of the strip together. In this version, however, the flexagon is created by cutting a slit in the shape of a cross in the center of the paper, and folding it up to create the illusion of a woven form. The Windmill Flexagon is very simple to flex, but it does offer an intriguing mystery: Exactly where is the that illusive windmill pattern concealed?

Begin by folding the paper into the Windmill base (see page 18), then unfold it completely.

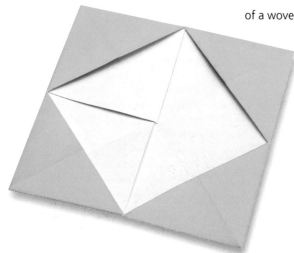

◁

The Windmill Flexagon is both a flexible toy and an intriguing puzzle.

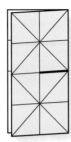

1 Unfold the Windmill base, then fold the paper in half vertically.

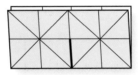

2 Cut along the crease marked with a thick black line only. Cut through both layers. Try to make the cut as accurately as possible.

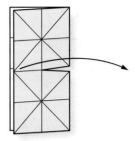

3 Undo fold 1.

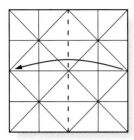

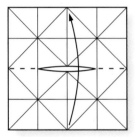

4 Fold in half horizontally.

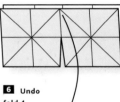

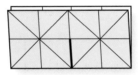

5 Cut along the crease marked with a thick black line only. Cut through both layers.

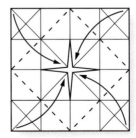

6 Undo fold 4.

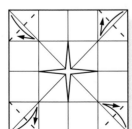

7 Fold each of the corner squares in half, then unfold.

8 Fold all the corners to the center.

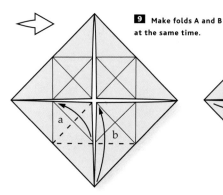

9 Make folds A and B at the same time.

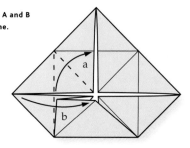

10 Make folds A and B at the same time.

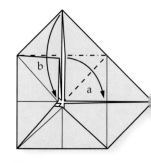

11 Make folds A and B at the same time.

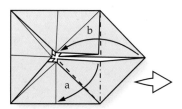

12 Make folds A and B at the same time.

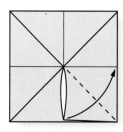

13 Rearrange the loose flap like this.

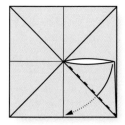

14 Tuck this loose flap inside the pocket.

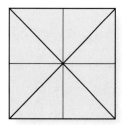

15 Turn over.

16 Fold all four flaps outward to the corners.

17 Fold the pointed flaps away into the pockets in front of them. Make sure the points do not get bent, and that they go all the way into the corners.

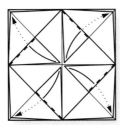

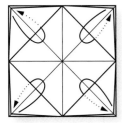

18 Fold the remaining set of flaps into the pockets behind them. Make sure the points do not get bent and that they go all the way into the corners.

19 The Windmill Flexagon is finished.

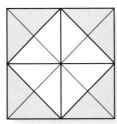

The Flexagon
Windmill Challenge

CHALLENGE 1

Can you discover how to flex the flexagon to find a face that looks like this?

The solution is on page 57.

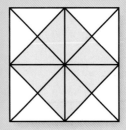

CHALLENGE 2

Can you discover the pattern of the Windmill concealed inside the folds of this flexagon?

A little lateral thinking is required.

The solution is on page 89.

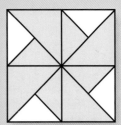

P-P-Pig

Designed by David Mitchell

Paper

You can make
P-P-Pig from any
kind of paper and in
any color—but pink
is probably best.

P-P-Pig is an idiosyncratic design. It is made in three incredibly simple sections that slot together, from tail to nose, to produce a model that somehow screams "I'm a pig!" whichever way you look at it. (Just so long as you don't look too long or too carefully, that is.)

This is a naive style of paperfolding, in which the essential details of the subject are merely hinted at rather than modeled in detail so that the design exists as much in the imagination as in the folding, and it is known as minimalist origami. However, P-P-Pig is somewhat unusual, even for a minimalist design.

◁

P-P-Pig is an idiosyncratic but instantly recognizable design, made in three parts which slot together from tail to nose.

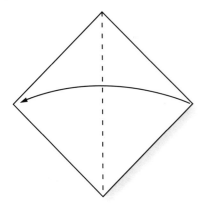

1 Fold in half diagonally.

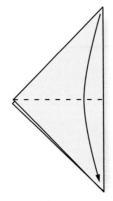

2 Fold in half again.

3 Fold all three sections to this stage, then follow steps 4 through 9 to turn one section into the tail and hind legs.

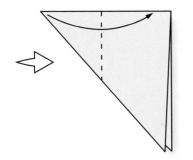

4 Look at step 5 to see what the result should look like.

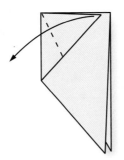

5 Look at step 6 to see what the result should look like.

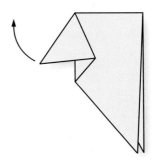

6 Undo folds 4 and 5.

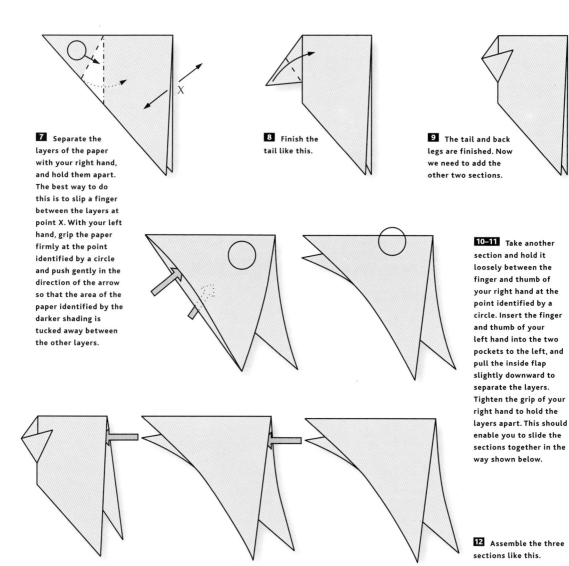

7 Separate the layers of the paper with your right hand, and hold them apart. The best way to do this is to slip a finger between the layers at point X. With your left hand, grip the paper firmly at the point identified by a circle and push gently in the direction of the arrow so that the area of the paper identified by the darker shading is tucked away between the other layers.

8 Finish the tail like this.

9 The tail and back legs are finished. Now we need to add the other two sections.

10–11 Take another section and hold it loosely between the finger and thumb of your right hand at the point identified by a circle. Insert the finger and thumb of your left hand into the two pockets to the left, and pull the inside flap slightly downward to separate the layers. Tighten the grip of your right hand to hold the layers apart. This should enable you to slide the sections together in the way shown below.

12 Assemble the three sections like this.

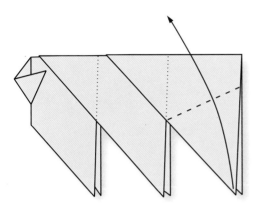

13 Make this fold in the top layers only.

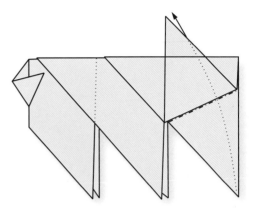

14 Fold the rear flap upward behind the model so that the tips of both flaps line up exactly.

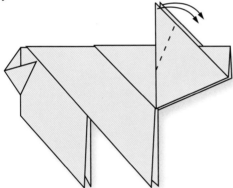

15 Fold the tips of both flaps forward to form the ears.

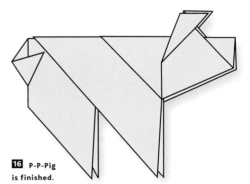

16 P-P-Pig is finished.

The Pencil

△
**Pencil is a simple
yet effective design
created using the
contrast between
the white and colored
sides of irogami paper.**

The Pencil is a modern design, but no one now seems to remember who designed it. This style of origami—in which the contrasting colours of the two surfaces of the paper are used to create a simple image—is called "drawing with paper," a description that is particularly appropriate to this design.

The Pencil is a particularly delightful design because it is so easy to vary. The instructions show you how to fold the design from a 4 x 1 rectangle, but it will also work well with many rectangles of other proportions. You can make a stubby pencil by beginning with a slightly shorter rectangle, and a thin pencil by beginning with a longer one.

Paper
The Pencil should
be folded using
irogami paper.

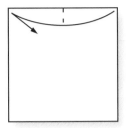

1 Mark the center of the top edge of the paper with a short crease.

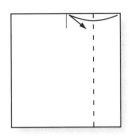

2 Use the short crease to locate this fold.

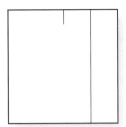

3 Cut along the crease to separate the two parts of the paper.

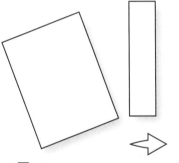

4 This piece is no longer required.

5 Fold in half vertically, then open out.

6 This fold forms the lead of the pencil.

7 Turn over.

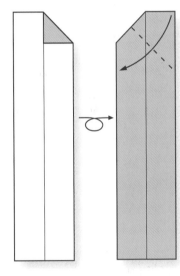

8 Line up the outside edges to locate this fold.

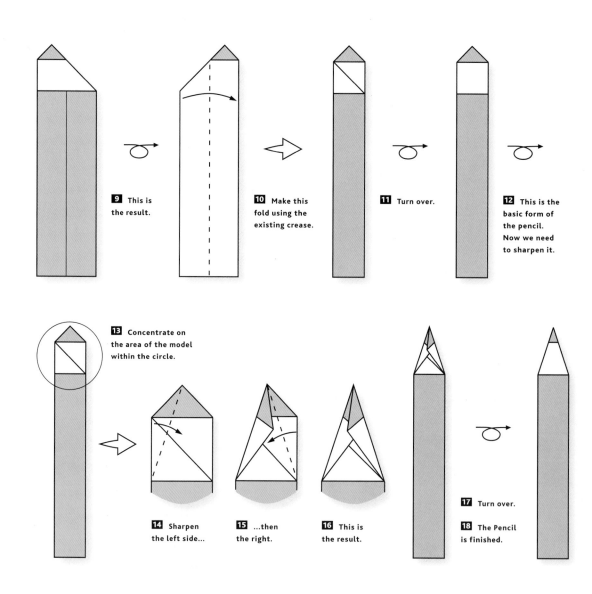

9 This is the result.

10 Make this fold using the existing crease.

11 Turn over.

12 This is the basic form of the pencil. Now we need to sharpen it.

13 Concentrate on the area of the model within the circle.

14 Sharpen the left side...

15 ...then the right.

16 This is the result.

17 Turn over.

18 The Pencil is finished.

The Flexagon Windmill Challenge

Here is the first solution.

HOW TO FIND THE SECOND FACE

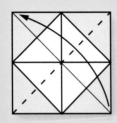

1 Fold in half diagonally.

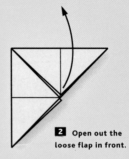

2 Open out the loose flap in front.

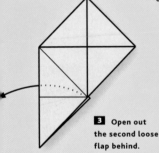

3 Open out the second loose flap behind.

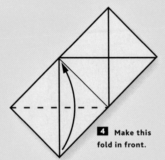

4 Make this fold in front.

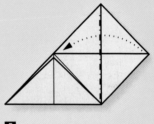

5 Make this fold behind.

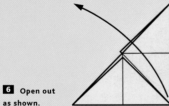

6 Open out as shown.

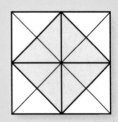

7 This is the second face. You can reverse these moves to return the flexagon to its original appearance. There are several other ways to achieve this transformation.

Merlin and Santa

Merlin designed by Oliver Zachary; Santa designed by Paula Versnick

△ ▷

Merlin and Santa are both excellent examples of the minimalist "drawing with paper" style of origami design.

Paper

Merlin and Santa should both be folded using irogami.

Merlin and Santa are excellent examples of minimalist origami design, executed in the "drawing with paper" style. It is fascinating to see how different the approaches of two designers working in the same style can be.

In traditional origami all the folds are located with geometrical precision, but modern origami sometimes requires one to locate a fold by eye alone— known as a "judgment fold." The slightly skewed geometry of Merlin is based on such a fold (step 3). It may take you several attempts to get the placement exactly right.

Some minimalist designs are more extreme than others, and they don't come much more extreme than the twofold Santa. Most people will understand and appreciate Merlin, but Santa is definitely for those with specialized tastes.

Merlin

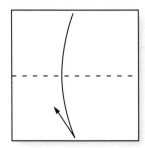

1 Fold in half horizontally then unfold.

2 Fold in half vertically then unfold.

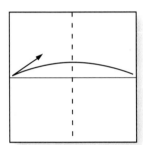

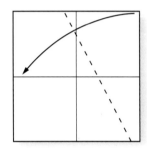

3 Locate this fold by placing the top righthand corner on the horizontal crease, just a little short of the lefthand edge. Look at step 4 to see what the result should look like.

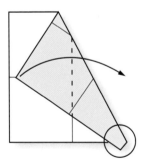

4 Make this fold along the line of the crease made in step 2. Crease firmly but don't try to flatten the rest of the paper.

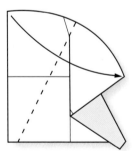

5 Line up the edges to locate this fold.

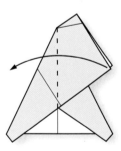

6 Fold both layers across to the left.

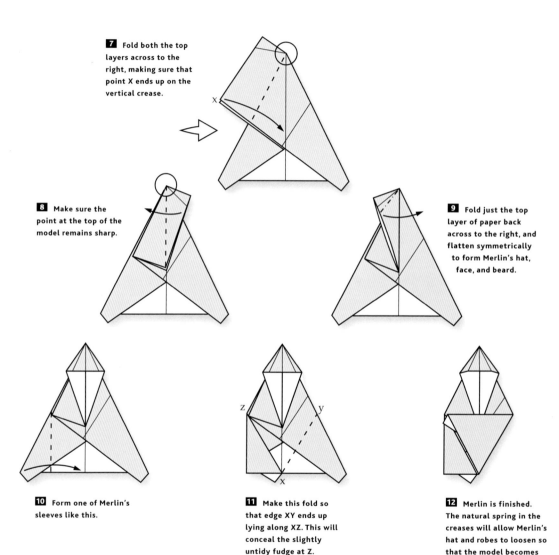

7 Fold both the top layers across to the right, making sure that point X ends up on the vertical crease.

8 Make sure the point at the top of the model remains sharp.

9 Fold just the top layer of paper back across to the right, and flatten symmetrically to form Merlin's hat, face, and beard.

10 Form one of Merlin's sleeves like this.

11 Make this fold so that edge XY ends up lying along XZ. This will conceal the slightly untidy fudge at Z.

12 Merlin is finished. The natural spring in the creases will allow Merlin's hat and robes to loosen so that the model becomes slightly three-dimensional.

Santa

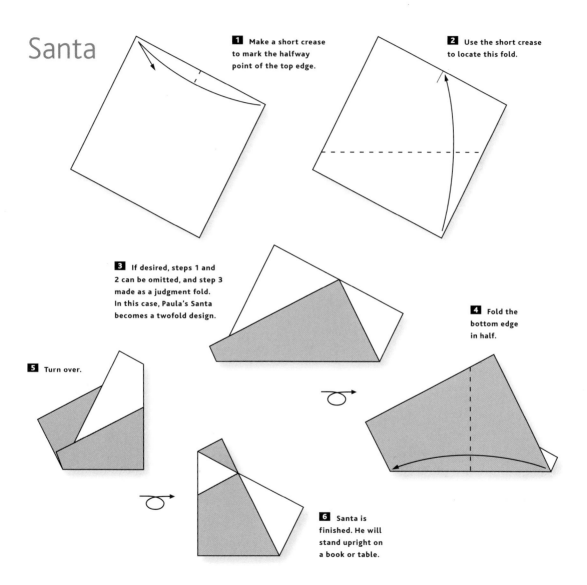

1 Make a short crease to mark the halfway point of the top edge.

2 Use the short crease to locate this fold.

3 If desired, steps 1 and 2 can be omitted, and step 3 made as a judgment fold. In this case, Paula's Santa becomes a twofold design.

4 Fold the bottom edge in half.

5 Turn over.

6 Santa is finished. He will stand upright on a book or table.

Dogfish

Designed by David Mitchell

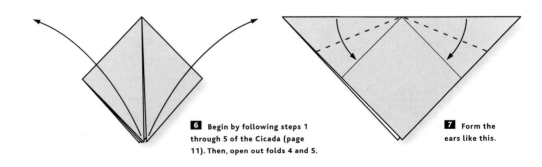

△

Dogfish is two designs in one, both extremely easy to fold. It begins as a dog and ends as a fish.

Paper

Dogfish should be folded from irogami.

Like the traditional Kabuto/Goldfish combination, this design begins as one model and transforms into another. In this case, though, the design is a modern one and so no cuts are involved.

Both the dog—well, perhaps more of a puppy really—and the fish are very basic minimalist designs, so a little imagination is called for, as well as some quite delicate folding.

6 Begin by following steps 1 through 5 of the Cicada (page 11). Then, open out folds 4 and 5.

7 Form the ears like this.

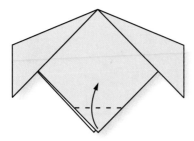

8 Make this fold in the front layer of paper only.

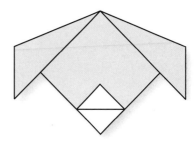

9 This is the dog. Follow the next four steps to transform him into a simple fish.

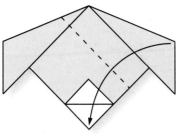

10 Make sure you crease this fold firmly.

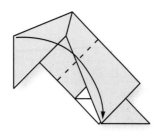

11 Make sure you crease this fold firmly as well.

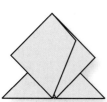

12 Rotate 90 degrees clockwise.

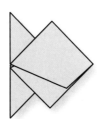

13 Turn over.

14 This is the fish.

Shipwreck

Designed by Oliver Zachary

Paper

Shipwreck looks more realistic if folded using fairly stiff, dyed paper, perhaps in a rusty brown color. Failing this, almost any kind of paper will do. You could try using brightly decorated irogami for a surreal effect.

Shipwreck is one of the strangest origami models ever devised. It is made in four very simple pieces that can be arranged to represent the bow, foredeck, deckhouse, and funnel of a wrecked ship, positioned as if they were protruding above the surface of the sea. The effect is enhanced if you place the model on a piece of blue or green paper.

▽

This origami model combines four easily assembled pieces to suggest a rusting hulk protruding from the sea.

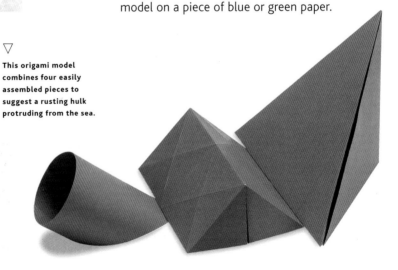

The Bow

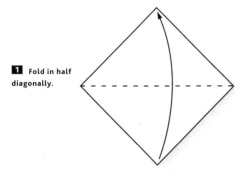

1 Fold in half diagonally.

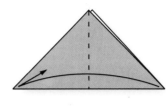

2 Fold in half again, crease firmly, then open out so that the two halves are at right angles to each other.

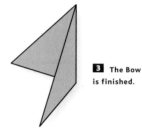

3 The Bow is finished.

The Foredeck

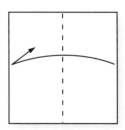

4 Fold in half vertically.

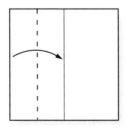

5 Fold the lefthand edge onto the vertical crease.

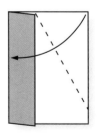

6 Look at step 7 to see the result of this fold.

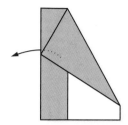

 Undo fold 5.

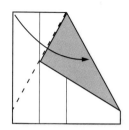

8 Align the outside edges to locate this fold.

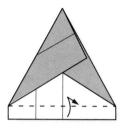

9 Make sure this crease lies parallel to the bottom edge.

10 There are four separate folds in this step

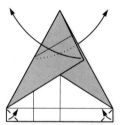

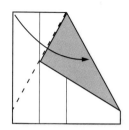

11 Remake fold 9 using the existing crease.

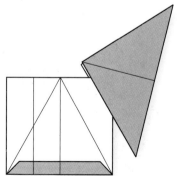

12–13 Use the Bow section as a template to help you make the next two creases.

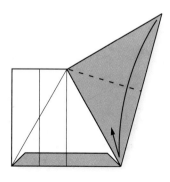

14 Make this crease in a similar way.

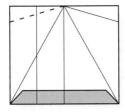

15 Lift the flaps up at right angles.

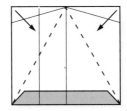

16 Turn over and fit to the Bow as shown.

17 The flaps of the Foredeck fit into the holes in the Bow.

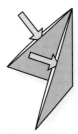

18 When inserting the flaps of the Foredeck into the holes in the Bow, you must make sure that the ends of both flaps slide around edge XX (in opposite directions). This holds the assembly together.

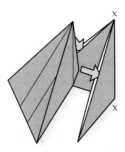

19 This is the result. The Bow and Foredeck assembly is finished.

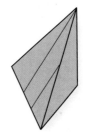

The Deckhouse

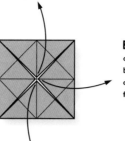

20 Begin with steps 1 through 9 of the Windmill (see page 19–20) but without turning the paper over between steps 6 and 7. Undo folds 7, 8, and 9 of the Windmill.

21 These creases will be used in steps 23 and 24.

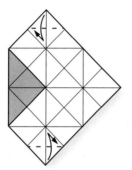

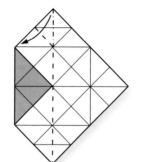

22 The model will become three-dimensional as you make this fold.

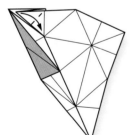

23 Make this tiny fold to lock the layers together.

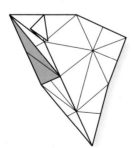

24 Turn the model around and repeat steps 22 and 23 at the other end of the paper.

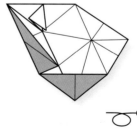

25 Check that your model looks like this before moving on.

26 The Deckhouse is finished.

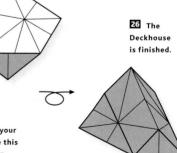

The Funnel

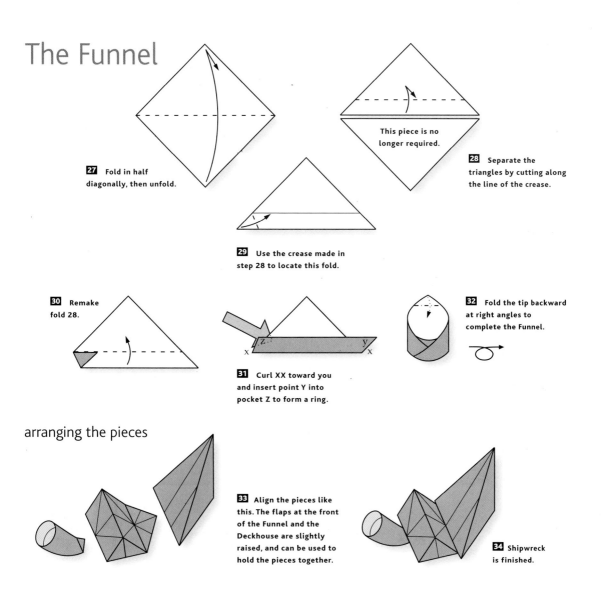

27 Fold in half diagonally, then unfold.

This piece is no longer required.

28 Separate the triangles by cutting along the line of the crease.

29 Use the crease made in step 28 to locate this fold.

30 Remake fold 28.

31 Curl XX toward you and insert point Y into pocket Z to form a ring.

32 Fold the tip backward at right angles to complete the Funnel.

arranging the pieces

33 Align the pieces like this. The flaps at the front of the Funnel and the Deckhouse are slightly raised, and can be used to hold the pieces together.

34 Shipwreck is finished.

Bric-a-brac

Designed by David Mitchell

△

Bric-a-brac is more than just a model of a boat. It is not only a means of transport but also the journey itself.

Paper

Bric-a-brac should be made from dyed paper.

Bric-a-brac is a simplification of the famous traditional model known as the Chinese Junk, which—despite its name—was probably a representation of a gold ingot. Folded paper ingots were (and occasionally still are) folded and burned as part of a traditional Chinese funeral.

Although Bric-a-brac is an interesting form in its own right (and will even do service as a toy boat if you stabilize it by dropping a few pieces of gravel, or perhaps a small coin, into the hold), the real point of the design is the enjoyment (or possibly frustration) one derives from the folding sequence, particularly the remarkable transformation effected in steps 28 and 29. As in so much of origami, how you travel is frequently more important than where you finally arrive.

First, follow steps 1 through 5 of the Windmill. You can use a standard Windmill base, but you will find it much easier if you incorporate steps 6a through 6d, as shown.

6a Begin by following steps 1 through 5 of the Windmill (page 19). Then, use the lefthand quarter crease to locate this fold.

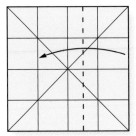

6b Unfold.

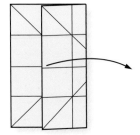

6c Repeat fold 6a in the opposite direction.

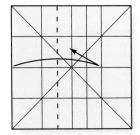

6d Turn over, then continue with steps 7 through 15 of the Windmill before returning to step 16 here.

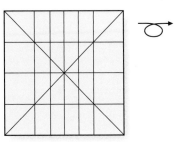

16 Rearrange the positions of the flaps like this.

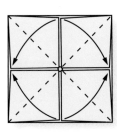

17 Open out the top two layers only.

18 Crease these folds firmly.

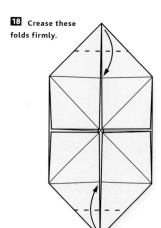

19 Open out the folds made in step 18.

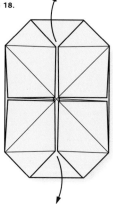

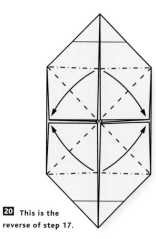

20 This is the reverse of step 17.

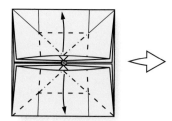

21 Concentrate on making the fold shown by the arrow. All the other folds will automatically collapse into place.

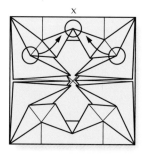

X

22 This picture shows the collapse underway. All the points identified by circles end up at point X.

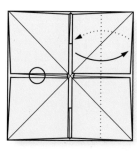

23 Pick the model up. Hold it between finger and thumb at the point identified by a circle. With your other hand, swivel the righthand half of the model backward through 180 degrees. The axis of rotation (the crease you made in step 6a) is marked by the dotted line.

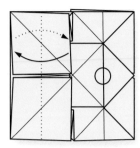

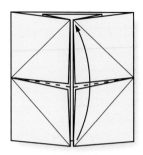

24 Swivel the lefthand side of the model backward in the same way.

25 Turn over.

26 Fold in half from bottom to top, being careful not to crush the corners of the flaps closest to the center as you do so.

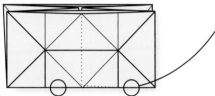

28 Repeat step 27 on the lefthand side of the model.

27 Pick the model up. Hold one side of the base in either hand at the exact points identified by circles. Begin easing out the hidden layers by gently moving your right hand in the direction of the arrow. The righthand side of the model will become three dimensional as you do this. This maneuver is difficult, and you must employ patience and practice to complete it without tearing the paper.

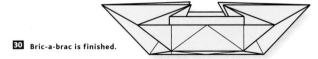

29 Squash and spread the base of the hull.

30 Bric-a-brac is finished.

Nichola's Box

Designed by David Mitchell

Paper

Nichola's Box should be folded using dyed paper. Use green paper if you want to combine the base with the lid to produce a floral effect.

Nichola's Box is an attractive open-topped container that can be used to hold pot pourri, paperclips, peanuts, or possibly paper cranes (although you would need a large box to hold a thousand of them).

The Floral Giftbox shows you how to make a lid to fit this box. Together, the lid and base form an attractive container in the form of a calyx and flower.

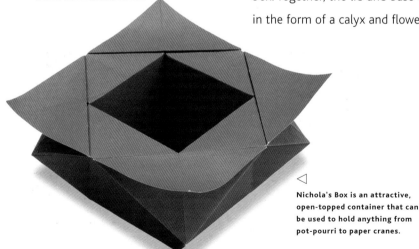

◁
Nichola's Box is an attractive, open-topped container that can be used to hold anything from pot-pourri to paper cranes.

6a Begin by following steps 1 through 5 of the Windmill (page 19). Then, use the lefthand vertical quarter crease to locate this fold.

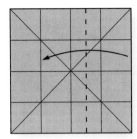

6b Open out.

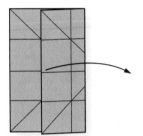

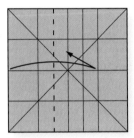

6c Repeat fold 6a in the opposite direction.

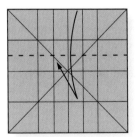

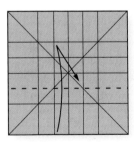

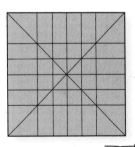

6d Use the lower horizontal quarter crease to locate this fold.

6e Repeat fold 6d in the opposite direction.

6f Turn over, then continue with steps 7 through 15 of the Windmill (pages 19–20).

16 This is the
Windmill base.

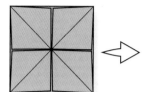

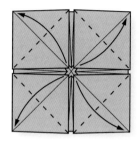

17 Fold all four flaps
outward to the corners.

18 Fold one of the
central points outward.

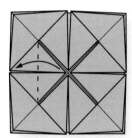

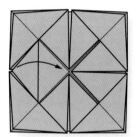

19 Unfold step 18.

X

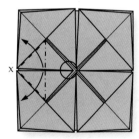

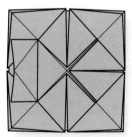

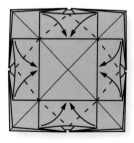

20 Make these folds
simultaneously, using the
creases you made in step
15. The point identified
by a circle ends up at X.

21 Repeat steps 18 to
20 on the other three
central points.

22 This is the result. Fold
all eight flaps inward.

23 There is a pocket below each of the large flaps identified by a circle. Fold the eight small flaps into these four pockets.

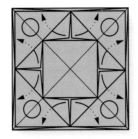

24 Turn over.

25 The model is now upside down. The base of the box is formed from the top layers of the model by squeezing the sides of each corner together in turn. The small central square that forms the bottom of the box rises up in front. Step 26 shows you how to do this.

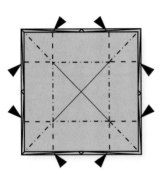

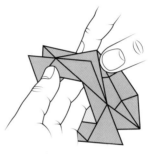

26 Insert two fingers inside the box to open up the layers, then use the thumb and forefinger of the other hand to squeeze the corner into shape. Do this with each of the corners in turn. All the creases you need are already there. Some of the small flaps formed in step 22 may slip out of their pockets as you do this. It is a simple matter to tuck them in again afterward.

27 The result should look like this. If you like, you can curl flaps a, b, c, and d upward to resemble the leaves of the calyx.

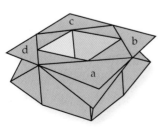

28 Nichola's Box is finished.

The Floral Giftbox

Designed by David Mitchell

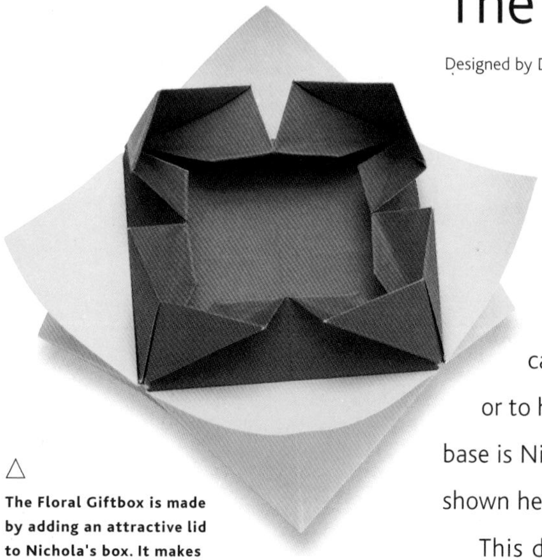

△

The Floral Giftbox is made by adding an attractive lid to Nichola's box. It makes an ideal presentation pack.

Paper

Both parts of the Floral Giftbox should be folded using dyed paper. If you want the giftbox to look like a flower, use green paper for the base (the calyx) and a brightly contrasting color for the lid (the bloom).

The Floral Giftbox is an attractive container that can be used for packaging any small but special gift, or to hold favors at a wedding. It is made in two parts: the base is Nichola's Box, and instructions for making the lid are shown here.

This design is particularly easy to vary. You might, for instance, like to try the effect of slipping an unfolded square of a second color inside the center of the lid. This second square needs to be one-eighth of the size of the square you fold the lid from. Try it and see if you like the result. Then experiment with your own ideas.

1 Make, then open out, each fold separately.

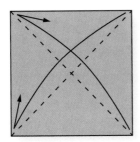

2 For the most accurate result, make these folds in the order a, b, c, d.

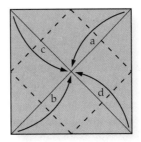

3 Turn over.

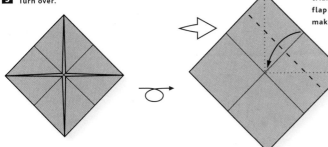

4 The dotted line marks the position of a hidden triangular flap. Allow this flap to flip forward as you make the fold.

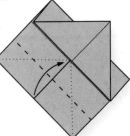

5 Repeat fold 4 on the other side of the model.

6 Undo the folds made in steps 4 and 5.

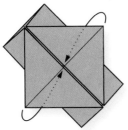

7 Repeat folds 4 and 5 in the opposite direction.

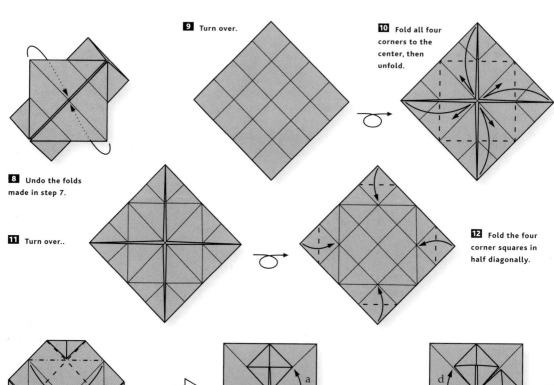

8 Undo the folds made in step 7.

9 Turn over.

10 Fold all four corners to the center, then unfold.

11 Turn over..

12 Fold the four corner squares in half diagonally.

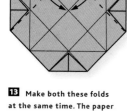

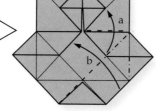

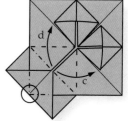

13 Make both these folds at the same time. The paper will collapse into the shape shown in step 14.

14 Make fold a, then fold b, being careful not to flatten the paper until both folds have been made. Allow the hidden triangular flap to flip forward as you make these folds.

15 Make folds c and d, then flatten the paper so that the point identified by a circle ends up in the center. Let the hidden triangular flap flip forward as you make these folds.

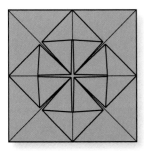

16 This is the result. Work around the model flattening all the creases.

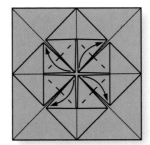

17 Fold the central points outward as shown.

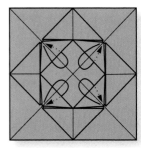

18 Tuck all four flaps away between the layers.

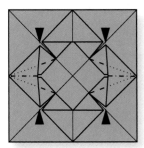

19–20 Gently add the new creases by squashing each side of each internal corner in turn.

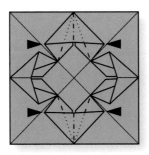

21 The lid is finished.

22 Insert the flaps at each corner of the lid into the pockets marked by arrows here. If you encounter any resistance, it will be because the small flaps already present inside these pockets are not lying completely flat.

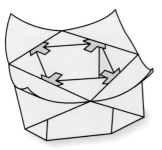

23 The Floral Giftbox is finished.

Octagonal Wreath

Designed by David Mitchell

▽

The Octagonal Wreath is made by combining eight modules, each folded from a small square of paper. Glue is not required.

The Octagonal Wreath is made by combining eight identical pieces, or modules, each of which is folded from a separate square of paper. This is called "modular origami," and is becoming increasingly popular because of the amazing results that can be obtained.

For best effect, you should use four squares in each of two contrasting but complementary colors. All the squares must be the same size, and small squares work best. You can obtain four small squares by cutting a large one into quarters.

If this wreath is folded using bright red and green paper, it makes a charming ornament for a holiday tree.

1 Fold in half diagonally.

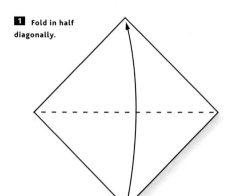

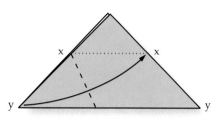

2 Make this fold so that edge XY lies along the imaginary line XX, which is exactly parallel to the bottom edge YY.

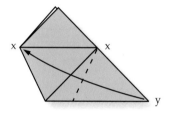

3 Fold XY up to lie along XX in the same way.

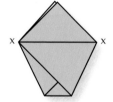

4 If necessary, adjust the edges that lie along XX until they are exactly the same length, and lie exactly on top of each other.

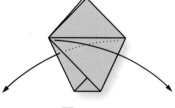

5 Open out folds 3 and 4.

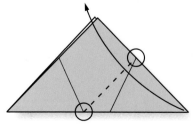

6 Once this fold has been flattened, all the edges at the righthand side of the model should line up exactly. See step 7.

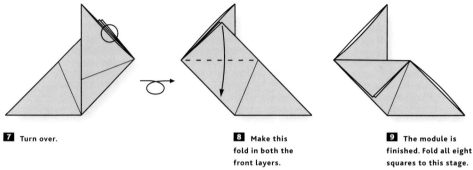

7 Turn over.

8 Make this fold in both the front layers.

9 The module is finished. Fold all eight squares to this stage.

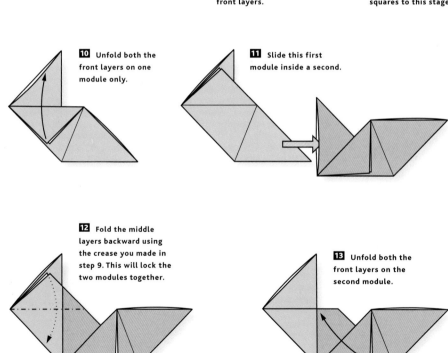

10 Unfold both the front layers on one module only.

11 Slide this first module inside a second.

12 Fold the middle layers backward using the crease you made in step 9. This will lock the two modules together.

13 Unfold both the front layers on the second module.

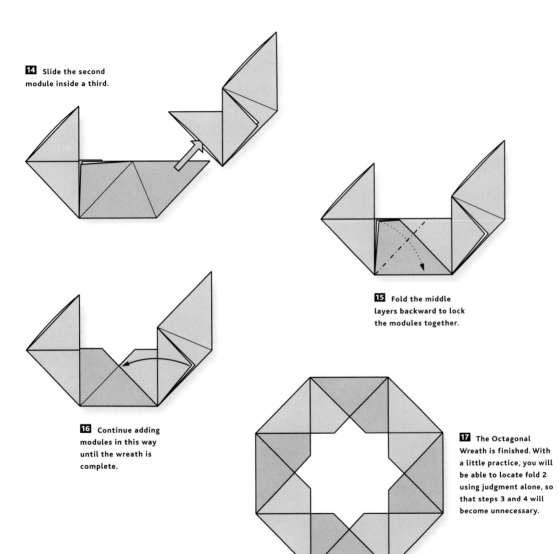

14 Slide the second module inside a third.

15 Fold the middle layers backward to lock the modules together.

16 Continue adding modules in this way until the wreath is complete.

17 The Octagonal Wreath is finished. With a little practice, you will be able to locate fold 2 using judgment alone, so that steps 3 and 4 will become unnecessary.

The Vice Versa Star

Designed by David Mitchell

△

The Vice Versa Star can be used as a decoration or to frame a photograph of your favorite friend, sister, pet, or hero.

Paper
The Vice Versa Star can be made from any kind of paper.

Like the Octagonal Wreath, the Vice Versa Star is made by combining eight simple modules. The folding geometry of the two designs is essentially the same, but there the similarities end. In the Octagonal Wreath, the modules form a solid octagon surrounding a hole in the shape of a star with eight points. In the Vice Versa Star, these elements are reversed and the modules fit together to form a solid star with eight points surrounding an octagonal hole.

For best effect, you should use four paper squares in each of two contrasting but complementary colors. All the squares must be the same size, and—again—small squares work best. You can use this modular star as a decoration or to frame a photograph of your favorite friend, or pet.

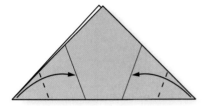

7 Begin by folding all eight squares through steps 1 to 5 for the Octagonal Wreath. Next, fold each corner to lie on the center of the diagonal crease. You should be able to do this accurately enough by eye alone.

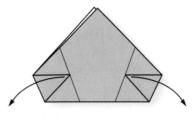

8 Undo the folds made in step 7.

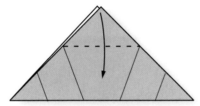

9 Make this fold in the front layer only.

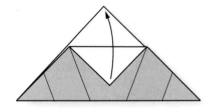

10 Undo the fold made in step 9.

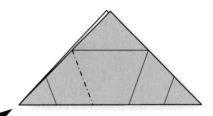

11 Turn this corner inside out so that it ends up between the other layers.

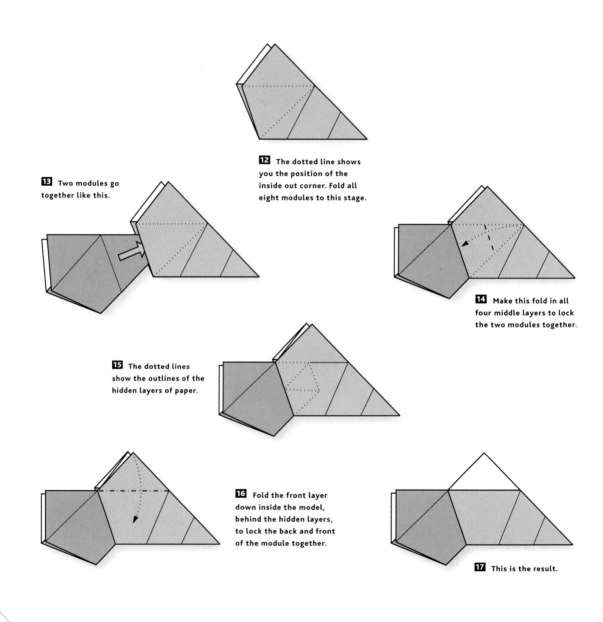

12 The dotted line shows you the position of the inside out corner. Fold all eight modules to this stage.

13 Two modules go together like this.

14 Make this fold in all four middle layers to lock the two modules together.

15 The dotted lines show the outlines of the hidden layers of paper.

16 Fold the front layer down inside the model, behind the hidden layers, to lock the back and front of the module together.

17 This is the result.

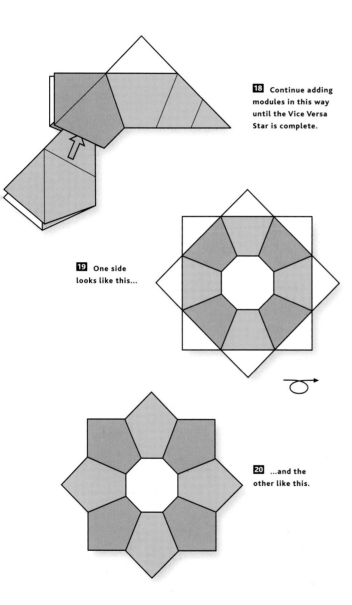

18 Continue adding modules in this way until the Vice Versa Star is complete.

19 One side looks like this...

20 ...and the other like this.

The Flexagon Windmill Challenge

Here is the second solution.

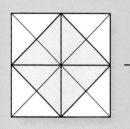

1 Begin from this face.

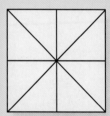

2 Hold the flexagon in front of a light source to reveal the pattern.

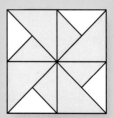

3 The windmill pattern is revealed.

Hat, Boat, and Star of Wonder

Star of Wonder designed by Oliver Zachary

Hat, Boat and Star of Wonder are a wonderful sequence of linked folds that combine the elegance of traditional origami with the freshness of the new.

Paper

Hat and Boat are best folded from dyed paper or paper that is printed on both sides. Star of Wonder can be folded using any kind of paper.

There was a time when every child knew how to fold a paper Boat. Nowadays, it has been overtaken by the ubiquitous paper dart, but it is still worth folding; the wonderful final move is so simple that even a young child can succeed at the first attempt. Unlike the Boat, the Hat (from which the Boat is made) has maintained its place in the popular imagination.

The Star of Wonder—an octahedron with a pyramid attached to each face—is one of the fundamental forms of modular origami, and there are many different ways to make it. This method uses twelve modules and produces a wonderfully robust result. Each module is folded from a rectangle of approximately the proportions shown. The exact proportions are not critical, but make sure that all your rectangles are the same size. For best effect, use four sheets in each of three contrasting but complementary colors.

The Hat

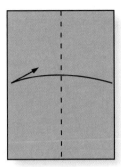

1 Fold in half vertically, then unfold.

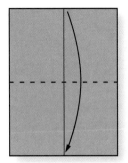

2 Fold in half horizontally.

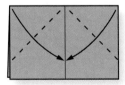

3 Feed both top corners onto the vertical crease.

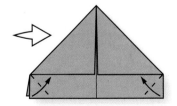

4 Make these folds in the front layer only.

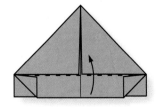

5 This fold holds the front of the hat together.

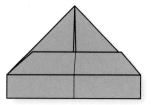

6 Turn over.

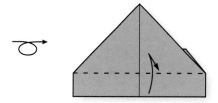

7 This crease helps to locate the folds made in step 8.

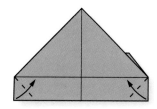

8 Repeat step 4 on this side of the model.

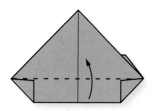

9 Repeat step 5 on this side of the model.

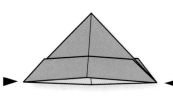

10 This is the hat. Squeeze the left- and righthand corners together to open. Try on for size.

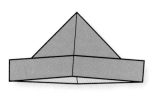

If you don't want to go on to make the Boat or Star of Wonder, a simpler version of the Hat can be made by omitting steps 4, 7, and 8.

The Boat

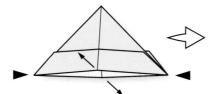

11 Continue squeezing the corners together until they meet in the center. The result should look like step 12.

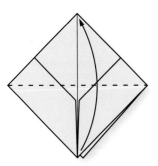

12 This fold is made in the front layers only.

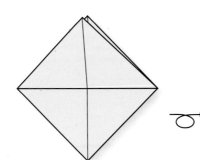

13 Turn over.

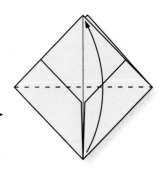

14 Repeat fold 12 on this side of the model.

15 Gently squeeze the left- and righthand corners together until they meet in the center. The result should look like step 16.

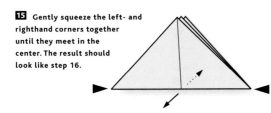

16 Take hold of the model at the points identified by circles (one in each hand) and pull them apart gently. The boat will take shape.

17 Finish the boat by gently curving the sides. The point in the center of the boat is traditionally known as the sail (though it is difficult to see how it would catch the wind).

Star of Wonder

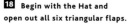

18 Begin with the Hat and open out all six triangular flaps.

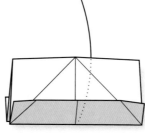

19 Bring the back half of the model into view.

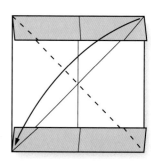

20 Make sure this fold is made accurately through all the layers.

21 Interweave the internal flaps (inside the layers at the corner identified by a circle) to lock the back and front of the module firmly together.

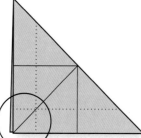

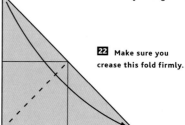

22 Make sure you crease this fold firmly.

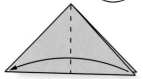

23 Make sure you crease this fold firmly too.

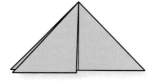

24 Turn over.

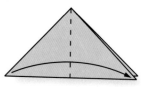

25 Repeat fold 23 on this side of the model.

26 Spread the points.

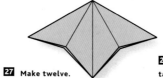

27 Make twelve.

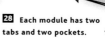

28 Each module has two tabs and two pockets.

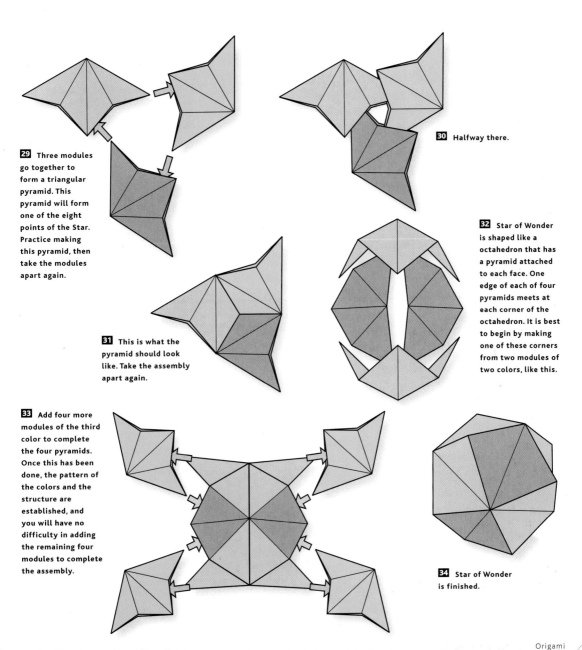

29 Three modules go together to form a triangular pyramid. This pyramid will form one of the eight points of the Star. Practice making this pyramid, then take the modules apart again.

30 Halfway there.

31 This is what the pyramid should look like. Take the assembly apart again.

32 Star of Wonder is shaped like a octahedron that has a pyramid attached to each face. One edge of each of four pyramids meets at each corner of the octahedron. It is best to begin by making one of these corners from two modules of two colors, like this.

33 Add four more modules of the third color to complete the four pyramids. Once this has been done, the pattern of the colors and the structure are established, and you will have no difficulty in adding the remaining four modules to complete the assembly.

34 Star of Wonder is finished.

Acknowledgements

A book like this is a team effort. My thanks are therefore due to everyone who has contributed their ideas, talent, and professionalism but particularly to Rebecca Saraceno, who always listened.

My particular thanks are also due to Paula Versnick, Polly Smith, and Oliver Zachary for generously allowing me to include their fine designs and to my wife, Lyn, for being there or not being there, whichever kind of help I needed at the time.

Oliver Zachary kindly undertook to double-check all the facts, diagrams, and folding sequences. Any remaining errors are therefore his alone.

GOING FURTHER WITH ORIGAMI

There are origami clubs in many countries which arrange conventions and publish regular magazines and collections of interesting new designs. The two main English speaking clubs are Origami USA and the British Origami Society, both of which are non-profit making organizations, run solely by volunteers. Both organizations began as purely national societies but now have membership from many different countries. Here's how to contact them.

ORIGAMI USA

15 West 77th Street

New York, NY 10024-5192

USA

www.origami-usa.org

THE BRITISH ORIGAMI SOCIETY

3 Worth Hall

Middlewood Rd

Poynton, SK12 1TS

England

www.britishorigami.org.uk